Sports Stars

PETE ROSE

"Charlie Hustle"

By Ray Buck

 CHILDRENS PRESS, CHICAGO

Cover Photograph: Steve Schwartz
Inside photographs courtesy of the following:
Steve Schwartz, pages 6, 16, 28, and 34
George Robarge, pages 9, 13, and 24
Chuck Solomon, pages 15 and 26
George Gojkovich, pages 18, 22, 38, and 40
Bryan Yablonsky, page 20
Ira Golden, pages 30, 36, and 42

Library of Congress Cataloging in Publishing Data

Buck, Ray, 1947-
  Pete Rose "Charlie Hustle"

  (Sport stars)
  Summary: A biography of the baseball player for the
Philadelphia Phillies whose goal is to break Ty Cobb's all-
time major league record for base hits.
  1. Rose, Pete, 1941-   —Juvenile literature.
2. Baseball players—United States—Biography—Juvenile
literature. [1. Rose, Pete, 1941-   . 2. Baseball players]
I. Title. II. Series.
GV865.R65B82 1983   796.357'092'4 [B] [92] 82-23482
ISBN 0-516-04329-3

    3 4 5 6 7 8 9 10 11 12 R 90 89 88 87 86 85 84 83

Sports Stars

PETE ROSE

"Charlie Hustle"

Did Pete Rose really grow up?

Growing up usually means slowing down. Pete Rose doesn't know what the word "slow" means.

He is more than 40 years old. But he still plays in the dirt. Baseball is his magic-carpet ride. Baseball keeps him young.

His headfirst slides are still his trademark.

His bat is still his best friend.

His nickname is Charlie Hustle.

His father taught him, "Never walk when you can run." So, Pete runs when pitchers give him a base on balls.

Pete has a flair for baseball. It oozes from his uniform. He stretches singles into doubles. That's just his style.

Pete Rose wears No. 14. He plays first base for the Philadelphia Phillies. You can pick him out of a crowd. He's the superstar with the dirtiest uniform.

Pete's next goal is to break Ty Cobb's all-time major-league record for base hits—4,191. This would make Pete the top hitter in baseball history.

He says he won't stop hustling until the record is broken.

Pete took 3,869 hits into the 1983 season. He needed 322 more to catch the legendary Cobb.

How long will that take?

Pete has averaged more than 193 hits a year for 20 years in the big leagues. So, he should break Cobb's record during the summer of '84.

By then, Pete will be 43 years old.

No sweat.

"Age doesn't mean anything to me," he says.

Pete loves baseball. He doesn't like to sit down. Since 1970, he has missed only nine games.

Ty Cobb, the Georgia Peach

"If I took a day off," he says, "I'd be sluggish."

Pete is a human tractor. He's tough. Once he played six weeks with a broken toe! He just cut a hole in the side of his right shoe.

Some fans call him a "hotdog" because he plays baseball with his nose in the dirt. Those fans don't live in Philadelphia. Phillies fans think Pete is "colorful" . . . and very, very good.

Pete Rose refuses to be so-so. He learned that from his father.

"My father was the most important person in my life," Pete says. "He pushed me all the time. If I went two-for-four, he'd tell me I should have gone three-for-four. If I went three-for-four, he would tell me I should have gone four-for-four."

Pete singles to left center.

Pete's father, Harry, was a great amateur football player in Cincinnati. He played until he was 42 years old.

"I guess I'm my father in the next generation," Pete says.

Harry Rose died in 1970.

"If it wasn't for my dad loving sports," Pete says, "he might never have passed that love along to me. I keep trying to follow in his footsteps."

When Pete's father spoke, Pete listened.

"Winning was his baby," Pete says. "He told me to go at baseball the same way I go at life."

Pete now passes along this special love for playing and winning to his son, Petey.

Pete gives "high" fives to his fans.

"I've never seen a 12-year-old who can hit like Petey," Pete says proudly. Petey Rose has been a bat boy for the Phillies. He wears a Philadelphia Phillies uniform just like his dad.

The great hitters in baseball have always had something in common. Great eyes.

Pete Rose can stand at home plate and watch a pitch traveling 90 miles an hour. He can tell if it is a fastball, slider, or curve. He looks for the "red dot." That means it is a fastball.

Swing early!

Here is Pete's secret. There are 108 stitches on the cover of a baseball. The way the pitcher grips the seams makes either a "red dot" or "mostly white" pitch. But only a great hitter like Pete Rose can see it.

"Whatever Pete says, I'll buy," says Sparky Anderson. Sparky was Pete's manager with the Cincinnati Reds.

When he faces a new pitcher for the first time, Pete will take two strikes "to see what he's got."

Pete knows all the tricks. He starts every game with a clean bat. That way he can see where the ball makes contact when he swings— early, late, or right on target.

Hitting is an art. Pete Rose is an artist.

Pete grew up in Cincinnati. He was good in all sports. But he always wanted to be a major-league baseball player.

Pete's dream came true when he signed a pro baseball contract with the hometown Reds in 1960. He was excited. But he had to spend three years in the minor leagues before he got his big chance.

Pete hustles to first base.

In 1963 Pete became the second baseman of the Reds. He was an instant star. The baseball writers named him the National League Rookie of the Year.

Pete played 16 years with the Cincinnati Reds. It was a mutual love affair.

But times have changed. And so has baseball.

Owners now spend a lot of money to get free agents to change teams. In 1979 Pete became a free agent. And baseball became "Let's Make A Deal."

The Pittsburgh Pirates wanted Pete. They offered him race horses.

The Atlanta Braves wanted Pete. They offered him part of a cable TV business.

The Philadelphia Phillies wanted Pete. They offered him a team that could win.

Baseball has always been the most important thing on Pete's list. He had become the first "singles" hitter to earn $1,000,000 a year. Usually only home-run hitters were paid that much money. In 1978 he was making $800,000 a year with the Phillies.

But Pete kept hustling. He was still Charlie Hustle.

"I don't worry about money," he says. "I play the game of baseball for fun."

The Philadelphia Phillies were a new challenge for Pete. It was the first time he ever played baseball for a team outside Cincinnati.

Pete had already proved himself to be an All-Star at second base, third base, left field, and right field with the Reds. Now he was asked to learn a new position—first base.

No sweat.

In two years Pete was leading the Phillies to their first World Championship. It was Pete's fifth World Series.

No matter what, Pete always tries to give his best.

In three years Pete had become the National League All-Star first baseman by a vote of the fans. This set a major league record: five different All-Star positions by one player.

Pete Rose is never too old to stop learning.

"I study the best players," he says. "When I wanted to know more about playing third base I talked two hours one day to Brooks Robinson. You are never too old to learn."

Pete is a baseball player bursting at the seams. There is no such thing as a quiet afternoon with him. Baseball is more than a job. It is an outlet for Pete to work off his energy.

Pete talks to John Stearns, the Mets catcher.

He likes to talk almost as much as he likes to swing a bat. This makes him very, very popular with reporters.

Pete is also a good sport. He has been "roasted" many times by baseball players and movie stars. "I'm burnt," he jokes.

TV commercials? He makes them look easy. Standing in front of the camera, Pete has told millions of TV viewers, "A man likes to smell like a man."

A candy bar has even been named after him. It is sugarless and full of energy. "It took us 38 formulas to get the thing to taste good," Pete says proudly.

He wears his hair in a reddish-brown, and some gray, shag. When he runs, it looks like a lion's mane. He plays tennis. He makes public appearances. He drives fancy cars.

Pete Rose does everything except grow old.

He isn't real big, but he is muscular. Pete is 5 feet, 11 inches tall and weighs a bulging 203 pounds. He stands in a crouch to bat. He chops singles for a living.

Astroturf is another one of his friends. Pete hits line drives that skip across the hard, artificial surfaces. They roll and roll.

But Pete was getting hits seven years before Astroturf was introduced in Cincinnati. The Reds played on grass at Crosley Field until 1970.

Pete's first major-league hit came on April 13, 1963. The pitcher was Bob Friend of the Pittsburgh Pirates. Pete got a triple.

Since then, 2,888 of his 3,869 hits have been singles.

Pete will be the first to admit he doesn't have the blazing speed that most other "singles" hitters have. He runs hard, not fast.

So he has to look for other advantages.

Pete began switch-hitting when he was nine years old. Mr. Rose made a deal with Pete's first coach: "Let Pete switch-hit and I won't take Pete away on any family trips during summer vacation."

The coach smiled and naturally agreed.

Pete would practice a lot on his own. He was always a manager's dream. He still is.

Pete's saddest season in the majors was 1964. His very first manager, Fred Hutchinson of the Reds, grew sicker and sicker. He died that year of cancer.

"It broke my heart," Pete recalls. "We were watching Fred Hutchinson die inch by inch, game by game . . ."

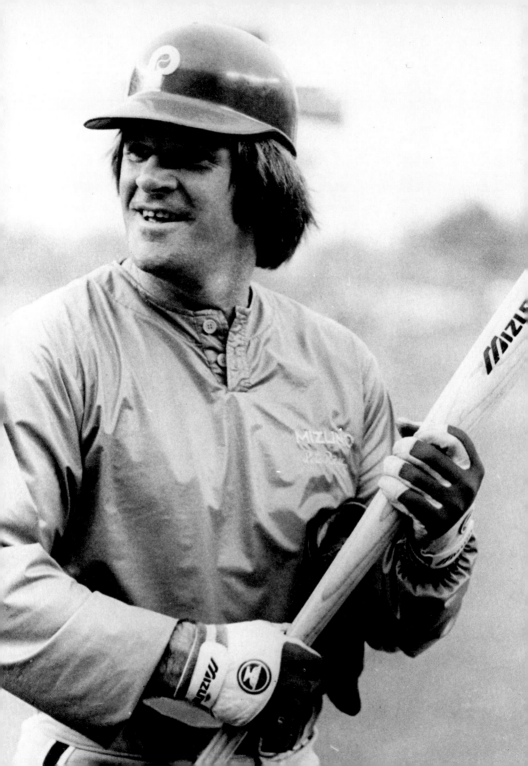

Almost 20 years later, Pete is trying to become the No. 1 hitter in baseball history. He is a rare breed.

"I've always believed that if you are going to go out for something," he says, "you should go all out."

What makes Pete Rose want to break up a double play or take an extra base even when the score is 12-0?

Pride.

"Because I've done it so many times," Pete tries to explain, "for so many years."

It's a habit. And this Pete Rose Spirit is contagious. Just ask the other players on his team.

"It makes you ashamed if you give less," says former teammate Joe Morgan.

Pete plays one way—TO WIN.

"Winning is everything as far as I'm concerned," he says. "Just so long as you play clean and don't try to hurt anybody."

This is his lesson for kids today.

"If you're going to do your homework, you ought to try and get a good grade," Pete says. "If you're going to give 2½ hours to a baseball game, you ought to try and win. Someone's got to win. Someone's got to lose. So let the other guy lose."

Pete, himself, is the best example of what he says. He rose from a middle-class neighborhood in Cincinnati. He became the National League Player of the Decade for the '70s.

He still plays baseball with his nose.

Okay. Did Pete Rose really forget to grow up? Now you know.

CHRONOLOGY

1941	—Pete Rose is born on April 14.
1950	—At the age of nine, Pete plays Knothole baseball and learns to switch-hit.
1960	—Pete signs as a free agent with the Cincinnati Reds on July 8.

1963
April   —Pete gets his first major league hit—a triple.

October   —Baseball Writers of America select Pete as National League Rookie of the Year.

1973   —Pete is named National League Player of the Year.

1975   —Cincinnati beats Boston in the World Series. Pete hits .370 and is chosen Most Valuable Player.

1978
May   —Pete singles off Steve Rogers of Montreal on May 5 to become the 12th player to reach 3,000 hits.

July   —Pete sets a modern National League record by hitting safely in 44 consecutive games, June 14 to July 31.

November   —After playing out his option with the Reds, Pete is granted free agency.

December   —Pete signs with the Philadelphia Phillies for $800,000 a year.

1979
August   —Pete becomes the all-time "singles" hitter in National League history.

October   —Pete becomes the first player in major-league history to collect 200 or more hits in 10 seasons.

1980   —Playing in his fifth World Series, Pete leads Philadelphia to its first World Championship in baseball.

1981   —Pete sets another major league record by starting at his fifth different position in the All-Star Game.

1982   —Pete doubles off John Stuper of St. Louis on June 22 to pass Hank Aaron for second place on the all-time hit list with 3,772.

November   —Pete signs with the Philadelphia Phillies for more than $1 million.

DO YOU REMEMBER?

Can you answer these questions without looking back in the book? If you need some help, turn to the page number following the question.

1. What is Ty Cobb's record for base hits? (page 8)
2. What does Pete's son, Petey, do?   (page 16)
3. How did Pete play with a broken toe? (page 12)
4. Why can you pick Pete out of a crowd? (page 8)
5. Where did Pete get his love for sports? (page 14)
6. What does Pete do when he faces a new pitcher for the first time?   (page 17)
7. How does Pete play baseball?   (page 23)
8. What did the Phillies offer Pete?   (page 23)
9. Why was 1964 Pete's saddest season? (page 35)
10. What positions has Pete played?   (page 25)

Do you like to win the same as Pete Rose? Why or why not?

ABOUT THE AUTHOR

Ray Buck is a sportswriter for the *Houston Post*. His assignments include major-league baseball, pro football, and Wild West rodeos. He has covered four World Series and five Super Bowls.

He is the author of three other sports books. *Dave Parker: The Cobra Swirl* and *Carlton Fisk: The Catcher Who Changed "Sox"* are also part of the Sports Star series. *He Ain't No Bum* illustrates the cowboy philosophy and coaching ideals of New Orleans Saints coach Bum Phillips.

Mr. Buck formerly covered the Cincinnati Reds and was at the 1975 World Series when Pete Rose batted .370 to win the MVP Award. "Pete Rose is like you or me," says Mr. Buck, "except he will be remembered as the greatest hitter who ever lived."